DIANE WAKOSKI

The Archaeology of Movies and Books

BY DIANE WAKOSKI

Coins & Coffins (1962)
Four Young Lady Poets (1962)
Discrepancies and Apparitions (1966)
The George Washington Poems (1967)
Inside the Blood Factory (1968)
The Magellanic Clouds (1970)
The Motorcycle Betrayal Poems (1971)
Smudging (1972)
Dancing on the Grave of a Son of a Bitch
    (1973)
Trilogy: Coins & Coffins, Discrepancies and
    Apparitions, The George Washington
    Poems (1974)
The Wandering Tattler (1974)
Virtuoso Literature for Two and Four Hands
    (1975)
Waiting for the King of Spain (1976)
The Man Who Shook Hands (1978)
Trophies (1979)
Cap of Darkness (1980)
The Magician's Feastletters (1982)
The Collected Greed, Parts 1–13 (1984)
The Rings of Saturn (1986)
Emerald Ice: Selected Poems 1962–1987
    (1988)
Medea the Sorceress (1991)
Jason the Sailor (1993)
The Emerald City of Las Vegas (1995)
Argonaut Rose (1998)

DIANE WAKOSKI

ARGONAUT ROSE

BLACK SPARROW PRESS
SANTA ROSA · 1998

ARGONAUT ROSE. Copyright © 1998 by Diane Wakoski.

ACKNOWLEDGMENTS

These poems, some in slightly different versions, have appeared in the following publications: *Ann Arbor Museum's A Visit to the Gallery, Carolina Quarterly, Cream City Review, First Intensity, Many Mountains Moving, Michigan Quarterly, Orbis, Plum Review, Poetry International, Recursive Angel, Red Cedar Review, River City, Sierra Journal, Southern California Anthology, Southern Florida Poetry Review, Sun and Moon Press Calendar, Whaling Station,* and *World Poetry Online.*

I had hoped to be able to use Peter Green's new translation of Apollonius Rhodius' *Argonautica,* which was to be published by UC Berkeley Press in 1997, but the book was still not available when I compiled this text, so I have stayed with the slightly archaic but still charming old translation by R. C. Seaton and published in the Loeb Classical Library collection.

Black Sparrow Press books are printed on acid-free paper.

LIBRARY OF CONGRESS CATALOGING–IN–PUBLICATION DATA

Wakoski, Diane.
    Argonaut rose / Diane Wakoski.
       p.   cm. — (The archaeology of movies & books ; v. 4)
    ISBN 1-57423-046-8 (pbk. : alk. paper). — ISBN 1-57423-047-6 (cloth trade : alk. paper). — ISBN 1-57423-048-4 (signed cloth : alk. paper)
      I. Title.   II. Series: Wakoski, Diane. Archaeology of movies and books ; v. 4.
PS3573.A42A64   1997
811'.54—dc21   97-39060
                                                         CIP

this book is for my father, the sailor,
and for all the heroes and enchantresses
I have known

TABLE OF CONTENTS

THE MAP (Why the Journey Is Necessary)

SILVER LIGHT

QUANTUM WHOLENESS

SILVER APPLES

THE ARGONAUTS, HEROES & FRIENDS

ADVENTURES DURING AND BEYOND THE JOURNEY TO COLCHIS

HER GREAT ANGER

USING ORDINARY WAVES

QUANTUM REALITY #3

MEDEA, THE ARGONAUT ROSE

AND HERE THEY FOUND CIRCE

[CIRCE] LONGED TO HEAR THE VOICE

EPILOGUE

ARGONAUT ROSE

THE MAP

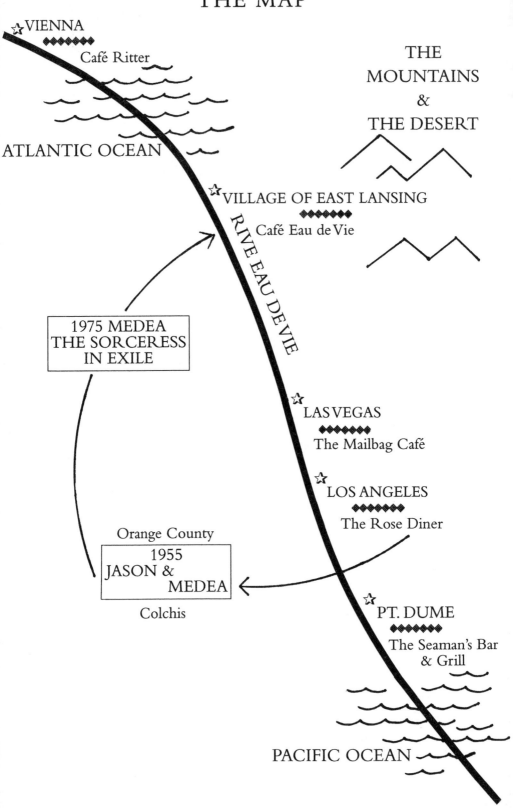

VIENNA
Café Ritter

ATLANTIC OCEAN

THE
MOUNTAINS
&
THE DESERT

VILLAGE OF EAST LANSING
Café Eau de Vie

RIVE EAU DE VIE

1975 MEDEA
THE SORCERESS
IN EXILE

LAS VEGAS
The Mailbag Café

LOS ANGELES
The Rose Diner

Orange County
1955
JASON &
MEDEA

Colchis

PT. DUME
The Seaman's Bar
& Grill

PACIFIC OCEAN

THE MAP

WHY THE JOURNEY IS NECESSARY

Such was the oracle that Pelias heard, that a hateful doom awaited him—to be slain at the prompting of the man whom he should see coming forth from the people with but one sandal. And no long time after, in accordance with that true report, Jason crossed the stream of wintry Anaurus on foot and saved one sandal from the mire, but the other he left in the depths held back by the flood. And straightway he came to Pelias to share the banquet which the king was offering to his father Poseidon and the rest of the gods, though he paid no honor to Pelasgian Hera. Quickly the king saw him and pondered, and devised for him the toil of a troublous voyage, in order that on the sea or among strangers he might lose his home-return.

Apollonius Rhodius,
Argonautica, Book I,
translated by R. C. Seaton,
New Haven/London 1912.

READING *BONJOUR, TRISTESSE* AT THE FLORENCE CRITTENDEN HOME FOR UNWED MOTHERS

for the late David Smith, my greatest mentor

I was empty as a new car, and
you brought me the novel, just published in English,
by the 17-year-old waif-like French girl, It was
1956. In 1957, the movie
was the first one to star the also very young
and waif-like Jean Seberg conniving
to drive her father's mistress, Deborah Kerr as the Parisian
Haute Couture, off a cliff near the Riviera.
I was lying in the hospital bed,
ready to face the sad cafes of exile
without cars
but not without love, and I
didn't read this book as if it were about selfishness,
willful children, speed or decadence,
though it is,
but as if it portrayed
        what?
men as betrayers, women
as poets, the singers. The sacrificers? I read it
as if it were about me, the girl with the extremely white
bare feet.
This isn't, I think
a very accurate perception,

but it prepared me to want to be
like Piaf,
to sing like Juliette Greco,
to live my life
as if only love, which to me WAS sex,
was the only whiteness, the only light, the only speed that
could articulate
beyond longing.

David, I walked in the dusty yard of The Home
memorizing Shakespeare's
"When in disgrace with fortune and men's eyes
I all alone beweep my outcast state."
I wanted
my Avocado-groves boyfriend to love me, I wanted him to
        wear
white bucks and have a crew cut like you, I wanted to look
        like Jean
Seberg and be rich
on the Côte D'Azur, I wanted
a David Niven playboy father to love me, but I was
one of those pale chunky girls from the orange groves,
disgraced and only reading books.
I read *Tess of the D'Urbervilles*
and *Jude the Obscure* while I was at that place,
books that have driven me through my life, whereas
I haven't once thought of Sagan's *Bonjour,
Tristesse*
since I flew off in my chariot drawn by dragons, not
off a cliff but into my Medea life.
Not once
until I watched the film on video this week
and found myself thinking
of you haunting your Point Dume house.
And of your beautiful French wife who defends me against

her sister who thinks I am an unnatural woman,
one who gave up her children
because they were simply flesh, and that was not the
    part of sex that
I believed in.
And of the past.

Do I still believe it is sex that has the only power to
    transform?
Do I still understand its urgent message that only
one moment
counts:
the one at hand?
Do I still believe that orgasm is the only clue
we have
to death?
Bare white feet, lily moon face,
a diamond wheel-of-fortune spinning out of control,
my once long hair cut into a silver cap
around my head,
just like the late fifties French haircut
of the legendary Jean Seberg?
Bonjour, Tristesse, hello sadness, hello death,
what lady sings that song now?

RIDING IN THE NEW TRUCK

for Steelman

I am wrapped in blue, a baby Robin
in her egg, Wonder Woman in the indigo night,
stars blinking on her bodice, an Angel Fish
near a coral reef in the Pacific, the water on some days
like sapphires brushing the cool burn of skin.
Robert shifts up and down, his black stick
slanted like the needle of a compass.
His blue Jimmy is smooth as a glove/
night swings in late, it's summer, the blue boy
is parked in our small-town driveway.

Take us to the desert
where our blue-as-a-storm-sky car has previously rolled:
bring us, like the argonauts to the California gold rush,
        chiming in
desert Moonflower light,
speeding past yucca-belled Joshua trees,
blue-belled, ringing
our way West.

THE ARGONAUT ROSE:
AMARYLLIS BELLADONNA

*for Joyce Benvenuto who said she did not
see how I could say that Darwin
represented "freedom from savagery"
when I depicted him torturing (sic) an
insect as he investigated the causes of a
firefly's glow*

(Note: In the jungle I would not survive. But I felt at
home, for the first time in my life the day I moved to
Manhattan. I am terrified of wind, of trees, particu-
larly of water, certainly of reptiles, but city streets are
not where I even imagine painful or deadly things
happening, though I am afraid of speed and crowds
and grew up in a small town, population 1900, so safe
that no one needed to lock her door.)

What is the history
of this arm of a red lily that towers
out of its January pot, ready to bludgeon anyone
with its axe-handled crimson blade?
That asserts itself
in bedroom, or kitchen, or even
on the front room coffee table
each winter, often with four trumpeting flowers
that fight against the darkness of winter

until they themselves shrivel into black rags?
How it has transformed my winter
to wake to it
each day,

but it reminds me too
that the dazzling humid jungles where parrot colors
are common and where
such tropic beauties, having
their sure origins,
are alien to me. Savage, Joyce,
with pulse. The blood of procreation even
seems like death in vivid colors
there. Do I
see
this flower in my drab mid-winter life
then
as death? One that fascinates me?
Its bulbs have been used for centuries as Kafir arrow poison.
Or is it more important that it helps me live
through the winter, and when it shrinks down
to a tatter of raven feathers
I know that we've successfully passed another winter,
that summer's on its way?

In fact, the Amaryllis flowers are blood,
removed from hurt and pain.

No sex,
no rape. The dawning of civilization.
Is it so sinister to loathe animals and insects,
while embracing man? Darwin was not torturing the firefly
when he dissected it living, even if
you believe insects

suffer as humans do. He was simply using it.
Not the "mis-use,"
that Olson chides us from,
but hierarchies of purpose. Logic
did not build
the universe; civilization means
fair
and equitable treatment, which
does not
mean a bug's life gets the same
consideration as
a woman's. The bug's life is used
to make human life better. The amaryllis
in my house gives me
joy
whereas seeing it
in a ferny South American jungle, amid humid ticking
        parasites
would only make me
cringe. I too, like so many foolish Christian missionaries,
long
to transform the jungle
into the garden.
To keep the change as long as life.
Yet, I know
all such efforts must revert,
after human death,
to savagery. This bulb, after its one florid showing,
will never again flower for me
so big,
or so beautifully.
And I believe too,
though I hate winter
and don't want to die,

that in some way,
excepting I will probably not recognize it,
I too
am somebody's Red Lion,
Amaryllis Belladonna,
my blood splashed to set aside one winter,
offered up as some one's flaming
Argonaut Rose.

SMALL BLOOD STAIN FOUND
AFTER MAKING LOVE

Revelation comes to everyone,
firefighters and old women burning toast.
You made love to the forest goddess whose hair wound in
        flaming
coils around her feet on the trail.
You wanted to take her with you, as the
image of the little curve of
blood on the sheet. But instead
you are sitting in a park next to a homeless sibyl wrapped
in newspapers, and feel empty,
as if the blood leaked out of your own body. But
where did it go?
She's not going to change her life,
and why should she?
She can only see you clandestinely;
as it is as if she is some book in a foreign language
that a reader would give away
if they knew what the text said. She can only
remain on the shelf,
untranslated.
Perhaps only our secrets
explain our lives, and to reveal any secret
is to lose all possible meaning?
Perhaps this stain is all
that's left
of a forest fire that rekindled Ponderosa

from a long-buried cone,
the crescent moon
she left behind shining
invisibly
on you every night?

SILVER LIGHT

The Mailbag Cafe

Dear Jonathan,

When I was a little girl, it was fairy tales that
entranced me, and one aspect of them was all the
golden things that princesses were connected with.
Little princesses had golden balls to play with.
Adolescent princesses had dresses embroidered with
golden thread, as well as pearls and rubies and
diamonds. And of course, when the princess married
the prince, then she won the golden crown.

For me oranges, the oranges that grew on the tree
next to our back door, the oranges ripening on the
trees in the groves surrounding all of our houses in

Southern California, they were the gold of daily life. And the spiders were black and gold. The poppies that bloomed in the spring, the California poppies, were golden. And as I got older I found out that California itself was called the Golden State.

So, I grew up thinking gold was the thing, perhaps even that I could be a golden girl. And yet my own destiny has proven to be silver, connected with the moon, my name Diane, moon goddess Selene, my hair always with more of a dusky silver cast than a golden one, and now that I am nearly sixty my hair is actually like moonlight, reinforcing the fact that my eyes have always looked Polish grey rather than Prussian blue.

As much as I loved the movies, growing up in Southern California, I was fearful of them, perhaps afraid of loving them too much, and so like the rest of the silver in my life, I tried to ignore the Silver Screen when I was young. But age has also connected me with that silver destiny, in some way that I am not still quite sure of. I think it all has something to do with water, the ocean, the tides, the way light is not just golden, as I have always preferred it to be. The way dark takes on a silver cast, or black turns silvery. The photograph negative. The x-ray. The movies I create in my head.

I remain yr lady of Silver Light,

Diane/Moon

RAY AND THE WHITE CAMARO:
A MEDITATION ON THE SILVER SCREEN

for metallic Ray

He was tall and lanky, the way I
think of cam shafts
though probably have the lingo wrong.
And from a town with a name I savored
like a taco: Chula Vista.

Examining the rented white
Camaro, Ray could have been a blond Elvis,
with his powder blue pants, and two-tone
jacket. Was this too much engine
for such a car?

How could even a guy who makes bad movies
    want to turn Lancelot into an itinerant rogue,
        one who'd never heard of chivalry, and didn't believe
            in honor? Talk about missing the point
            of the story!

Yes, don't panic; I might be changing the subject.

And now someone with millions
    has changed the ending
        of *The Scarlet Letter*

and let a prom queen play
     Hester Prynne!

Relax, there's a point to all this.

I know Robin Hood has fared worse, over the
     years, but he's like Santa Claus, not literature.
          Now Hollywood has turned Beethoven—I ask you
               Beethoven!—
                    into a Romantic lover instead of a composer.
               How can I bear the movies?

And books! do they assist me?

Now I am reading, *Past Imperfect,*
     about all the movies that get history,
          not just myth or literature, wrong.

Why can't they simply invent movies, the way we invent
ourselves?

All I want is fiction's veracity, poetry's truth.
No brother, surfer-blond,
fighting blues-fire would open this
smile-bright door for me, nor would
metallic Ray. I always opened my own door
and got into my car alone.

Me alone, walking in Dorothy's silver shoes?
     —changed by the movies into ruby slippers, all because
          they wanted to use Technicolor!—

Ray wouldn't drive
the white Camaro because it was

28

my car, rented when I first learned to drive
and visited my father in San Diego just before
he saw me on TV and died.

Ray with all the sun's light
shining out of his shellacked nails? He should have just
        stomped
his Elvis blue suedes on the gas pedal
and driven me to Rosarita Beach for the night.
Oh Ray, X-ray, not interested in Poseidon's horses.
    Ray, who didn't want to ride in my first car,
        with its excessive horsepower
            that white Camaro charger in 1969
                Ray, you are the movie that gets everything
                    wrong,
                you are the story
                    —*not your fault, mine entirely*—
                        in the sense that we write our
                        own stories:
                        You are the story, Ray,
                        of my blues-blood
                        late-driving
                        silvery
                        metallic
                        life

FISH STORY

for the sculptor

a fish as silver as the edge of dawn
lies on this crushed ice
at the Fulton Street Fish Market, your studio
nearby. I still believe
that sex is the true voice
of the body, not its great deceiver, I still
think I can capture you with bishops and rooks,
I still go searching for a voice
that would not invade your gray terrain, and I still think of
    you
thirty-five years after you caught me in
the laundromat in the Village,
a nymph I thought I was

Here, "still"
    means "yet,"
        not stillness.
Olson's song against mis-
use, this silver hook
still dangling
out of my old lip.

THE MISSING SANDAL

the reason that Jason gets sent off on the
journey of adventure to find and bring
back the golden fleece, is that his uncle
who has usurped the kingdom from his
father hears a prediction that he will lose
the throne by the hand of a stranger who
comes to town wearing only one sandal.
Then Jason arrives, having lost one of his
sandals, and he's quickly sent away with
the promise that he can have the
kingdom if he can bring back the golden
fleece. Everyone assures the king that
nobody can do this.

for all the Jasons

How could he just walk
into town,
wearing one sandal
and think we would not notice?
Especially with the silver
moon falling at night
and crashing like a helmet on the beach?

Why,
        after crossing the stream

that put silver knives and forks
into my California mouth
when he lost the sandal from his right foot,
didn't he take the other one,
with its straps of soft kid,
off?

Couldn't he see that we noticed,
narrowing our silver eyes?
After we shook his hand
with our silver gloves, couldn't he see that
we noticed?
Why didn't he think any stranger would have
been better coming barefoot entirely
than to hobble in, half shod,
even in gold?

And once he noticed, it was too late.
Heavy, heavy, with too late-ness,
we sent him off in a silver boat.
With silver breath, we hoped
he would not come back until
his hair too
was silver. But you can only
tell your own story.
In fact, I wasn't even there when this happened.

And his, Jason's story,
was a golden story,
a King of Spain story,
a Spanish galleons and treasure story,
a proud single gold sandal story,
while my story was
silver

silver
silver,
like dawn and metallic winter oceans,
the grey eyes of Medea
thinking she was stealing the gold for herself
and finding it did not belong to a silver woman.

But I didn't notice, either, with my silver eyes.
I didn't know anything but the beauty of leather straps
glowing with the sun,
as soft as tongues on his stealthy feet,
and when I met him he was wearing both sandals,
though I should have noticed something else. That his
        history
and fascination was all for gold, and I was the silver
woman, the sorceress of moonlight.

It's hard to imagine now
that my story was ever connected
to a stranger who came to town wearing
only one golden sandal.

But my story is the story of how the two, in fact,
do not complement each other:

silver and gold.

QUANTUM WHOLENESS

QUANTUM REALITY #3 (REALITY IS AN UNDIVIDED WHOLENESS)

Quantum wholeness is no mere replay of the old saw that everything is connected to everything else, no twentieth-century echo, for instance, of Newton's insight that gravity links each particle to every other. All ordinary connections—gravity, for one—inevitably fall off with distance, thus conferring overwhelming importance on nearby connections while distant connections become irrelevant. Undoubtedly we are all connected in unremarkable ways, but close connections carry the most weight. Quantum wholeness, on the other hand, is a fundamentally new kind of togetherness, undiminished by spatial and temporal separation. No casual hookup, this new quantum thing, but a true mingling of distant beings that reaches across the galaxy as forcefully as it reaches across the garden.

Nick Herbert
Quantum Reality:
Beyond the New Physics

SITTING AT HOPPER'S MARBLETOP TABLE

In Hopper's painting, she is drinking a cup of coffee;
she so white and the rest of the world
black with night, the white marble table
cool and unscarred. There is the moon in the form of
    flowers
and no one understands that the zebra is always
waiting outside the door. There is
a bubble on the coffee's surface, and
once she felt as if the sun gave her a glaze
that any lover would lick off, that anyone would want to
taste.

In the cafe, it is not a hat, but a cloche
of darkness that surrounds her
head, just as if
she often stopped the car
at an intersection and the urge just
to hold her head in her hands,
just to hold it and moan
overwhelmed her,
but then she thinks of the Pacific Ocean
and the curl of a wave,
She thinks of sitting on the Terrace at Point Dume with
    friends
under the blue awning,

she thinks of walking on the beach
and the way that the sand articulates each muscle
of the foot, of how beautiful
feet can be
when they are often bare, buffed
against sand, washed
with yes, the blue
Pacific.

Tonight the cafe is deserted, and hooded with her age.
She can hardly resist holding her head in her hands
in front of the few people, but she would not do that,
she would not do that. She has white legs
showing from under the table. Once they were tan
and once they carried her in and out of interesting places,
anxious to find the King of Spain, anxious to hear
        Beethoven
when she lifted the receiver of a phone. I know that the
        cup
holds tea, not coffee, its amber liquid
less potent, and she knows that if she just smiles,
and does not allow herself to feel

absurd

she will enjoy the evening,
as she walks home, through the small town
where the main street always reminds her
at night
of a Hopper painting. She will enjoy knowing life is only a
        doorway
to art, that it is an echo, a reminder, a suggestion,
at its richest, an innuendo. She knows this
though she has to work so hard

to get to the place
where balance occurs, where she can
push away the cup and saucer on Hopper's marble tabletop,
arise,
pass beyond the cafe door
to the zebra always waiting for her
outside.

HALLOWEEN COSTUMES

for Craig Cotter

He does his best
to understand her. Did He really walk
by her house when he was jack-o-lantern young
and look for lighted candy corn windows?
If they were lighted,
    it wasn't as He thought—
        to keep away bats
            and the neighbor's black cat—though she was
                probably
                sound asleep
                and it probably was
                her night-owl husband
                who was sitting there in the lighted eyrie,
                and he who would not turn out the lights until
                he went
                to bed around 4 a.m.
                    Lights for him,
                        so that he would not
                            stumble in the drunken
                            dark,
                    lights for her to substitute
                        for a life of radiance
                            she felt she once had lived.
Outside the midwest, He does the best

40

to understand her. Didn't he
ever see her zebra? Perhaps she is not so much
wondering why she has brought the zebra back, but why
it got lost in the first place?
Where did the zebra go
   when the naked girl got off its back?
      Did He ever see her when he walked past
         the lighted house, was she ever like
            Rapunzel, combing her long hair out of the eyrie
            window
            or was her husband the only one there
            photographing the dark in available light?
            She has no images from that time that are not
            reflections/
            but perhaps that is because she had not yet
            rediscovered the Hollywood her childhood
            should have offered her, or perhaps did, but
            which she rejected. Diana of the Silver Foot
            should have been Diane
            of The Silver Screen.

Near Hollywood himself, He does his best
to understand her. She offers him the third-hand story
of a diamond bullet-proof vest, the protection of the
         Russian royal family,
which did not save them, but the image of which
she thinks might save her. From which execution
   is she fleeing? Or is it only a story, so that she can
      claim royalty, pretend she might have been Anastasia
         more interesting in Hollywood than in History,
            wearing diamonds over her heart to protect
               her from The Motorcycle Betrayer, The
               Bluemoon Cowboy, The Pony Express Rider or
               The Homosexual Sheriff of Dry Gulch County

41

and finally lead her to
The King of Spain?

Out of her life, He
tries to understand her,
offers her his personal trust and anger,
tells her she is still in the house that looked
so empty to him, when He used to walk past it in the dark,
wondering at all the lighted windows in the middle of the
        midwestern
night,
    never seeing it as perhaps she might have felt it, like a
        neon-lighted casino in Las Vegas, a building of light
rising out of her own desert,
    she in the rooms where
        she is quite prepared to gamble away all the
diamonds, then
    ride away naked forever
        on her zebra.

ORPHEUS AND ROSES: A WOMAN'S MYTH

Why couldn't he bring her back?

No, the question should be:
"why didn't *he bring her back?"*

I know a woman who rides naked on her zebra, except
for a diamond bullet proof vest.
The zebra
also has diamonds
that throw light off his bridle like confetti.

The moon was the only wedding present
she asked for, but not one box
contained even its light. Still there were
rose petals, millions of rose
petals filling the cartons which bore legends like
"Microwave Oven," "Cast Iron Griddle," "Cuisinart
      Blades".
What happened to these bits of kitchenware,
and how did the boxes come to contain
rose petals? Or was it confetti?
Diamonds?
Yet she wasn't unhappy, even though she
did keep looking for the moon.

But he was unhappy: Orpheus.

He was unhappy. He didn't expect the moon,
but he also didn't want rose petals or a
bride who would never cook
or have children. He looked back to find
his mother, and when his bride saw
him looking, not for her but his expectations,
well of course she disappeared. She didn't even have to go
　　　away:
she simply dissolved.
Who can live forever with
disappointment?

And he didn't want to bring her back.
That's the answer.
Let's face it. He needed more than rose petals.
He was not interested in living on
moonlight. He had his
supper to sing for.
He was a man of substance;
there was so much of him.
And that's why
the Maenads tore him apart.
He bled as if he were covered with Georgia O'Keeffe
　　　poppies or
American Beauty rose petals.

EL CAMINO REAL (THE KING'S HIGHWAY)

For Jerry Rothenberg, who now lives in
Southern California where I no longer live

We transform the places we live.

Just beyond my oak trees, here in East Lansing, Michigan,
I imagine I can hear
the ocean of my childhood,
voices
like sequins from the jackets of Elvis, The King,
or Liberace
floating on these waves of Michigan green.

Only now you've multiplied
the voices, Jerry:
"Frank Mitchell's Horse-Songs" can be heard
"wwwn-ing" and "Nnnn-ing"
on the edges of cliffs still lined with purple ice plant.
Stevens did not have more siren voices
in his waves than you've added
to our Pacific:
  Satan in Goray,
  Arshile Gorky,
  Gertrude Stein,
  Tristan Tzara,
  the tormented from the Seven Hells of Jigoku
   Zoshi,

45

as well as your own voice
raised in sorrow and praise for all
spirited dead.

Right now I see nothing but the leaves of my yellowing
    oaks,
like gold coins floating on the autumn air,
when I look out my window
to the edge of this small back yard, but I know
you are out there, right on the edge of the Pacific Ocean
    which might
be as close as Grove Street, one block over.
It is there that
"White Sun, Black Sun"
cuts each diurnal movement
into long stemmed yellow roses,
rustling the tissue of their slim florist box.

Just as I drive down my main street in this mid-western
    town
whose yellow glowing street lights at night
give it the exactness of an Edward Hopper painting,
you turn daily
off El Camino Real,
the glittering bearded highway of the Spanish King.
My King of Spain
is an idea, an image of someone
searching—for a life which lasts, not just
a mirror life, but one filled with Birds of Paradise,
patio Cymbidiums and paper-exquisite winter lettuce.

I think,
to many of us,
you have invented that royal image, Jerry,

the power to travel anywhere, explore:
 the voice which floats on the waves like sequins,
 the voice which floats down from my oak trees like
  gold coins,
 the voice of phosphor, floating out of my mid-western
  street lights,
 the voice which is like a pumpkin,
 not the sun, but a golden moon,
 full, pollen-yellow, shaken and
 radiant with earthy
 big-seeded light.

1991 (revised 1997)

SILVER APPLES

The Mailbag Cafe

Dear Craig,

Making art is always an uncomplicated act, since nothing can be called art by its maker, only by those who observe it and perceive it as such. I suppose the same thing is true of love, though in both cases— making something you think of as art, or making love—paradoxically, one experiences a kind of ecstasy that is entirely unrelated to response, completion, or success. I believe the quest for art and/or love has occupied me entirely. I continue to think of this quest as a search for what William Butler Yeats ("The Song of Wandering Aengus") called "the silver apples of the moon" and "the golden apples of the sun".

Yrs from the Garden of Silver Apples,

DW

FALLING WOMAN LEAVING THE GARDEN

She runs on a chain of cities, only to
stagger, her feet pulled up
into the autumn flurry of paper.

The temptation of apples in her hands,
the silver foil of a candy wrapper
blowing against her foot,
dinosaurs reduced to metallic lizards
smelted somewhere around the globe.

I admire the way
she holds herself together,
how she finds the name of an apple
and uses it, like tinsel, to tie up a bundle
of old letters.

I also admire the fact
that she is alone and without any hesitation
about geography. The man who
offered her the Stonetosh
delineates her in black,
without desire,
while she only looks back
to pluck the apple by its silver stem. She is falling
out of love. A necklace of apple cores
around her neck like a large bunch of
silvered keys.

READING THE PHARMACIST'S DAUGHTER'S LETTERS

for Chase Twichell

Each one feels
like digging into a walled garden
to plant a silver apple

And the life—
it feels as if someone tall as poplars
led it. Silvery leaves, a body
trailing white water from swimming
naked, a red towel draped
over an oak chair,
in a white summer wickery room.
Someone who is never lonely
and owns thick towels
writes these perfect
letters
pasted around fresh transparent glass
bottles.
She
pours a little file of crystals
from a few. But most
are empty with glassy expectancy,
waiting for her long hand graceful as a spoonbill
to hold them
one by one,
while she writes each letter,

labeling them,
telling of a life lived with the smell of prescriptions,
as fresh as wet printer's ink,
sharp on a cut page.

THE BARN

a meditation inspired by
Adrienne Rich's "Diving into the Wreck"

She hides her American eyes
in her jeep
parked outside
the stylish old barn turned into
a theater. Her hands
like the branches of an apple tree fork onto
the steering wheel, and she almost bows her head
against this circle she controls,
as she does not control
the people in the barn,
. or
the forbidden man to whom
she wants
to make love. She
is not
the mermaid/merman
in the silver-gleaming, black
skin-diving suit;
she is not I,
nor I she.

Too far from water,
in this orchard night, she is driving, not diving into
a place where no one, whose name

appears in her old address book,
could possibly be. This man,
with a face like an apple, who gave
her once
an apple split in two, is inside
drinking cider and reciting poetry. But she leans
over her steering wheel in the dark,
and none of the actions of the rich diver
can help her. Even if she
fumbles for her knife,
loads a camera
or shines a headlamp onto the Book of Myths,
she will find it a book
she no longer knows
how to read.

I would like to
give her a silver key. In fact, I would offer silver
light from my own eyes if it might be of use; I
would show her a manuscript illuminated with silver
        apples,
but she wants the gold of his Argonaut
smile. How I understand that. She wants
the apple bough arms that rowed and needed
the Golden Fleece to be encircling her. She bows her
        head
over the steering wheel
of her four-wheel drive vehicle,
not knowing anymore
why she thought she'd find rebirth
in this barn, or that she there
might be offered a golden apple
by a hero.
I watch her despair, her crying in her

car at night, sympathize with her longing for
this man, but can do nothing.
Moonlight is solitary,
no substitute, only a reflection
from the sun's light; my own American eyes
light up
silver spaces.

NIGHT BLOOMING JASMINE: THE MYTH OF
REBIRTH IN BERKELEY, CALIFORNIA

It wasn't on Crete, but in the hills of Berkeley
where the Daughter disappeared. And forget crocus. It
was the pink rhododendrons, like festival lanterns
or sunsets over the bay, which attracted her.
Their season is the season of that town.
The Maybeck houses
with their brown woody, thrushy sides
grow like hedgehog mushrooms, out of the slopes.
She lives there, hidden all winter in one of them,
and then like Garbo going out for groceries
in her shades, spring
      with tulip trees and hawthorn,
      with azalea, the pinks and whites, not even her colors,
      not the girl in the swing ruffled with the beauty
      men do not know how
      to touch—spring
brings her out, could that be?

No, she is going for *The New York Times*, she is slim
in her dark clothes, she has cheek bones and ankles
that the screen will notice. She is not made to protest
war or the loss of free speech, she is made for a dark espresso
bar, a grocery
smelling of fresh pasta and tins of tomato paste,
the coffee bean store with vials and philters, and alchemical
ways of extracting aromas,

her foot in its thin shoe, entering the bakery,
the boulangerie, where long sticks of bread or round
    pannikins
of whole grain are waiting.

This is the town where poets lurk, and books contain
musical notes often stamped with gold leaf. It is the
place where you can learn that everything has a skeleton, a
    structure
of bones that is more important than the flesh, so
changeable, which covers them.

Corn bread here is
a sculpture of meal and moisture. Polenta a cake
stirred until the spoon stands alone in the mixture, where
soft things gain stiffness, it is the place where wine can be
    truly
conceived of, if not made, and it is where everyone learns
    to be
an architect.

I envy those who dwell in this city, the
bones of the world, I call them. Am a different
kind of Daughter than the Mistress of Chez Panisse,
or the woman who taught me I could not be a pianist.
Not elegant-boned, more a carapace,
I walked through the streets, wearing my own shades,
    disguised
as one of the young, oh so sad, bums, an alcoholic cloud
of Night Blooming Jasmine wafting from my moonlit hair.
You'd never know it was the city of rebirth—
a concept incomplete without a sojourn underground
coming first. I know what happens when you look back/
I'm not doing that. Some part of me never left;

I belong to the place
  like the Maybeck houses,
     the Edward Teller of the Atomic Bomb,
        the Greta Garbo women cooking
           in the fragrance of night blooming jasmine.

YELLOW BRICK ROAD

for Craig Cotter

No salad has ever tasted as good
as that one in the Beau Rivage, with the yucca bells
on top of it,
the one I ate when it was still
light one California evening,
and the Pacific Ocean across the
highway was pulsing along with the nostalgic piano notes
of Cole Porter.
Cynthia's fingers were Venus fingers,
pink-tipped and held like porcelain flowers
hovering over the petal-reality of the white yucca bells.

No, because every time I recall that moment,
I add to the savor of eating those flowers. You
still seemed like a boy to me, and Cynthia
a girl, a child bride,
one you had rescued from her piano-crushing husband.
We were sitting on the edge of Malibu,
and the three of us were sharing
our changing identities. Who could have known
that I would become the witch?
She was a lost princess
and you were someone searching for something
that sent you East of the Sun and

West of the Moon.

But now it seems as if we were all in different stories,
though we felt so much like we were in the same one that
    daylit evening
when we sat behind the bougainvillea of a terrace across
from Balboa's blue Pacific, and ate salads that were each
    topped
with yucca flowers. Desert flowers ironically offering us
succulence we needed?
Or was it only I who felt this,
since I am the one who has never stopped dining
on that most perfect salad?

THE ARGONAUTS, HEROES
& FRIENDS

Now when gleaming dawn with bright eyes beheld the
lofty peaks of Pelion, and the calm headlands were being
drenched as the sea was ruffled by the winds, then Tiphys
awoke from sleep; and at once he roused his comrades to
go on board and make ready for the oars. And a strange cry
did the harbor of Pagasae utter, yea, and Pelian Argo
herself, urging them set forth. For in her a beam divine had
been laid which Athena had brought from an oak of
Dodona and fitted in the middle of the stem. And the
heroes went to the benches one after the other, as they had
previously assigned for each to row in his place, and took
their seats in due order near the fighting gear. In the
middle sat Ancaeus and mighty Heracles, and near him he
laid his club, and beneath his tread, the ship's keel sank

deep. And now the hawsers were being slipped and they poured wine on the sea. But Jason with tears held his eyes away from his fatherland.

Apollonius Rhodius
Argonautica, Book I,
translated by R. C. Seaton,
New Haven/London 1912.

THE ESCORTS

When the actresses, like glove-shaped velvety bats trapped
in a room, hear their names called
and stand up, slightly blind in all the lights—
       even the glitter reflecting off their diamond earrings
              and bracelets—
and look desperately around the room full of twinkling
       celebrities,
knowing they have to flit up to the stage and receive this
       award, they are
shaking with unbelief: they've actually won!
and disoriented in the crowded room,
and with unfamiliar shoes, and dresses that
rest precariously on their bosoms,
heavy jewelry and somewhere in a costume with no
       pockets
a piece of paper on which is scribbled what they
hoped they'd have a chance to say
if they won,
there is always a moment when you think,
"Oh, my god, she's going to trip over someone! She's going
       to
stumble or fall" but then they are there,
those escorts in their traditional tuxedoes, black armed,
       white breasted,
young
Tyrone Powers or Clark
Gables, and instantly one arm is under the

winning arm of this actress or around her Scarlet O'Hara
    waist,
and they are moving as well as Fred and Ginger, so that she
    looks as if she
too floats
and he can steer her anywhere. How comforting
those young men
in tuxedos,
there always in just the right place,
efficiently escorting
those velvety girls
without panic
away from the crowd and out, up to
the freedom of the stage
where they fly off
into the oratory of gratitude and
acceptance.

Oh, that we should all have such tuxedoed-men
waiting for us when we panic,
trapped, feeling as if we are hanging upside-down
in a room where we don't belong.

BEAUTY

for Tim Lane

I never thought of him as beautiful,
but today he looked as tired as if he had fought a forest fire
    all night,
and he made me want to hand him a hot paper cup
of fire-fighting coffee,
though I know actually that he never drinks
that brew.
He's worried about
their car
that needs replacing,
and is exhausted as much from the stationhouse tedium
of being a house husband,
taking care of a toddler,
and the candleflame wish
that his wife, a special ed teacher didn't always
get assigned the worst, most incendiary jobs because
of her expertise.
He wants to tend her, even light a bonfire for her,
but working part time as a janitor
while he earns
a Master's degree, being a full-time
new father, knowing they can't
afford to replace their car which is almost totally
burned out and ready for the junkyard

gives him that look.

Yet he smiles at me, listens
to my tales filled with hot air,
and lovingly receives the gift of my fiery criticism.
He knows the disappointments
of the auto assembly line, his father a frequently
laid-off mechanic who still sent him through college on a
    blue collar ticket.
How I have always admired this man,
yet never seen him as beautiful—
his red-headed Irish grin, a rainy-day grin.
His fire, more like
a steady pilot light that almost no one but
the repairman ever sees. But today
his face seemed beautiful in its everyday fatigue.
He wore a blue mechanic's shirt
with a name, not his, on the pocket,
and he paced the room when I suggested ways to change a
    letter
he'd written. "I can't,
I don't want to
sell myself," he says. I smile and rewrite the paragraph for
    him.
After all, there are fires that are invisible and useful
and more important than those big ones
    often burning out of control,
        destroying acres of forest
            and all the houses, spotted owls and deer in their
                paths.
I think I saw that pilot light
glowing out of his face today,
keeping the stove ready for a meal
or the water tank full of hot water,

or the furnace ready to remove autumn's chill.

It surprised me,
fire-observer that I am,
that I had never seen it before.

DAVID & GEOFFREY

for the late David Smith and
Geoffrey Bankowski

The man who's dead
is the one we want to understand,
but of course that's the problem, like peaches that look so
     blushingly
good, but are hard and tasteless and only soften to bruises
     and
more tasteless pith—we can't taste death until
there's no way to communicate it.

Death must be tasteless, though dying
bitter. And nothing we say about death means anything
at all, except in terms of the living. So, sitting in this
     overstuffed chair
next to you in your leather jacket and flannel shirt doesn't
make me feel comfortable because you are
just like David, but rather it makes me feel at ease
because
I just remembered how few men
have needed me,
as you two have, and how I am the only one
who has ever known that.
No wonder I feel so
at home with you,

you who would do anything
for me,
you,
wearing the flannel shirt with
a nap soft as peaches,
though it's the leather jacket that reminds me
of the friend who so
un–understandably
needs me
no more.

THE RED SILK CLOTH AND THE PIKE STREET MARKET

for Eric Schmidt

A pile of salmon covering a table as big as our wooden
     terrace,
their scales like the silver
that wakes me up some nights,
the cloud-covered sky pulsing against
mushroom-skinned Oaks, the smoky puff
of a full moon behind them

And the green clash of Oriental vegetables, also piled up
on wooden slats and counters
that makes me know I will not return to sleep
for several hours. I find a red silk kimono to wrap around me
on full-moon nights, and in the downstairs living room
sit and wait for a low flat bowl of bouillabaisse
with its Oklahoma clay rust colored broth to reach into
the night.

What a good friend you've been to me,
and an inspiration,
shopping for free fish bones to make the Marseilles stew in
     Seattle,
serving me once in your fifth floor New York walk-up,
     bathtub-in-the-

72

kitchen flat
with no modern equipment, a gâteau Paris-Brest you'd
       made from scratch,
or bringing the giant mushroom, also orange as your
       bouillabaisse,
and the size of a soccer ball, as a house present when you
       came to visit us
in the Midwest. I
need friends in my life who connect to me via feasting. I
       still have
the big tin ground-pepper cans you mailed to The Feast
       Letter Project,
complete with black silk tassels and wrapped in the red silk
       cloth,
which now, after all these years,
is tacked on my bulletin board along with a photo of Tom
       Cruise,
Robert holding a Silver Salmon he caught, and an image
of the rings of Saturn.
Of course,
our first connection is always words
that represent any abundance we experience.
When the moon radiates my window
and I wake up beyond sleep,
it is not just my age that causes this phenomenon
but the long history of feast letters,
illuminated with the gold, crimson and lazuli of religious
       manuscripts.
The world is filled with places to worship
beginning with markets filled with great wooden tables of food.
And when I cannot sleep, it is as if I am starving
and though I may go downstairs, I never actually look at
       the cupboards or
refrigerator,

it is always a book I open, or a letter,
and feast on words until I am full and glowing,
and then the full moon that is my lettered life, instead of
    waking me,
joins me in the comfort of sleep.

GARDENIAS

for Norman Hindley

Norman, this summer
just as you left the lush swamp of Michigan, wearing
your Cap of Darkness jacket
and carrying your tarragon mustard and
the feather-light tin of husk-dry green peppercorns,
my potted gardenia
which had been sweating and covering itself
with buds, furled and wound-tight like turbans,
began to bloom.
                                    You who gave me
the weekly gift of gardenias
when we lived on Molokai
fired me with the desire to make my own white flowers
show their morning radiance
and jasmine the Michigan night with their scent.
But my apartment, always too dry and cool/
So, in their little tub they were given to
        the outdoor balcony and the real nights
and days of midwest summer.
Do you know that when each flower blooms
it opens one petal at a time
like the hands of a clock
moving
slowly

towards 12? Sometimes the opening seemed slower
    than it was;
I, used to the surprise of a plant suddenly
burst into bloom,
flowers at once
where previously there was nothing or only
the hidden.

        But, each gardenia
opens almost exactly like the
clock it emulates,
one petal, one hour, a second, a third,
from morning when there were only strips of white,
    till evening
when the whole wedding dress flower has extended
its toothy petals.

On Molokai, we
didn't have a Christmas tree
because they cost $50 apiece,
and besides it seemed bizarre and ugly
to be in a tropical land celebrating a season
which doesn't exist there.
Your son, Christopher, said to us
when he heard we had no Christmas tree,
"You mean you'll wake up Christmas morning
and there will be only
beer and wine bottles on your living room floor?"

No, there were gardenias too,
and the magnificent Birds Nest Fern
you lent us for our stay.
But, most of all, there was the promise
of our friendship,

of the celebration at your house
where the big gardenia bush grows.
The roast beef grilled to rare succulence,
the room full of Pamela's beautiful paintings,
and the unimportant Christmas tree and presents.
Now, we've celebrated mid-Summer together too.
With wine and poetry and more roast beef.
On your departure,
gardenias replace you in our living room.
Friendship
not just of holidays,
but for all seasons.

East Lansing
1979

MY FRIEND

(to) Michael Rossman

who named his son Lorca,
DNA'd his way through my life in those days,
playing his recorder as if he were goat-footed,
seducing slim nymphs who lived in the Berkeley hills
with his blue eyes and fat volume of Garcia
Lorca's complete works in Spanish.
He didn't know that
studying physics could have been
his ticket to poetry; instead
he stood in front of fire hoses picketing the House Un-
    American Activities
Committee and made me imagine
I had a brother who was a twin,
and that he could have been that brother.

I dreamed of eating
with silver, and wearing gold bracelets. Had neither, so
didn't have to learn about gold and silver—
how they don't mix. I played
the piano badly, with passion that probably
was almost marketable, and only regret now
that I didn't really become his twin,
study physics when I was young,
or cling to his friendship,

that young translator of Garcia Lorca,
so that today I might really have
had a brother, one who didn't
jump off a cliff or vanish
in the silver night.

ADVENTURES DURING AND BEYOND THE JOURNEY TO COLCHIS: BETRAYERS, DISAPPOINTMENTS AND FALLEN HEROES

But with the setting of the sun the wind left them, and it was by the oars that they reached Lemnos, the Sintian isle.

Here the whole of the men of the people together had been ruthlessly slain through the transgressions of the women in the year gone by. For the men had rejected their lawful wives, loathing them, and had conceived a fierce passion for captive maids whom they themselves brought across the sea from their forays in Thrace; for the terrible wrath of Cypris came upon them, because a long time they had grudged her the honors due. Oh hapless women, and insatiable in jealousy to their own ruin! Not their husbands alone with the captives did they slay on account of the marriage bed, but all the males at the same time, that they might thereafter pay no retribution for the grim murder. And of all the women, Hysipyle alone spared her aged father Thoas, who was king over the people; and she sent him in a hollow chest to drift over the sea, if haply he should escape. And fishermen dragged him to the shore.

... Now for all the women to tend kine, to don armor of bronze, and to cleave with the plough-share the wheat-bearing fields, was easier than the works of Athena, with which they were busied aforetime.

Apollonius Rhodius,
Argonautica, Book I,
translated by R. C. Seaton,
New Haven/London 1912.

QUANTUM THEORY #3 (REALITY IS AN UNDIVIDED WHOLENESS)

The essence of a local interaction is direct contact—as basic as a punch in the nose.

... On the other hand, the essence of non-locality is unpremeditated action-at-a-distance.

Nick Herbert,
Quantum Reality:
Beyond the New Physics

WANTING BEES

You are writing your
autobiography and
asking me to buy a copy. You sent an
order form in the mail.

But in the same letter
you said
you were tired of hearing
my decadent descriptions of soft-shelled crabs
eaten in New Jersey, or a blueberry tart
I made for my friends. What
about my
autobiography? Couldn't
you find the details
of my life
engaging
even for the space of a letter? When I

was a little girl, I wanted the bees
to sit on the yellow satin ribbons
combed into my blond braids,
and sometimes they did. I felt chosen
and would smile, nod my head:
the bee goddess.
But other children
ran away. "She has bees on her head!" they'd scream.
Cassandra, I was, even then.

HELMETS OF BRONZE

And on their heads they placed helmets of bronze, gleaming
terribly, and the blood-red crests were tossing. And half of
them rowed to turn, and the rest covered the ship with spears
and shields. And as when a man roofs over a house with tiles,
to be an ornament of his home and a defense against rain, so
they roofed over the ship with their shields, locking them
together.

> Apollonius Rhodius,
> *Argonautica, Book II*
> translated by R. C. Seaton,
> New Haven/London 1912.

*(Jason and his sailors preparing to fight the
battle against the birds of the island of Ares)*

He doesn't know that the freeway he rode
with his father twice a week
after his parents got a divorce
is an American highway offering
mythic adventure, that
little boys in our time
don't grow up to be cowboys or soldiers or even
mullet fishermen. He's

got man parts, but he knows no more than that little boy
riding in his father's Chevrolet with the windows rolled up,
        even
in summer; he likes to talk, has little to say, but his eyes like
Frisbees, throw their glances across the room—a game or
        missiles?—
he tells
us of the kid games he played
in that car, driving the regular route,
hating to leave his mother
but wishing that he could live with
his father. They are so damaged, these boys,
not even interested any more in toy soldiers or plastic
guns. Walk or ride, he doesn't know
what journey he could take
unless it's standing on a stage with a microphone and lots of
        girls
yelling his name. Why should he read poetry or think
        about
the voyage of the Argonauts? He thinks getting famous is
        what
it's all about, not the wisdom acquired
when we see kings and heroes fail.

I could tell him he's wasting his time,
but even that, he should somehow
figure out for himself. Surely all those trips
in his father's car, retracing the route between Detroit
        and
the suburbs, represent some kind
of modern journey?
Sometimes I see him, like a rooster, his hair a crest,
        coxcomb, a macho
target for others who are old enough,

failed enough
to carry
weapons.

SKATE BOARD

Rolling behind
the bus, hooked on
to the highway, the freeway
surfer never crashes,
never comes up blinking
with salt in his eyes.

Cypris, at the behest of Hera and Athena, speaks to her son, Eros, to persuade him to pierce Medea with an arrow of longing for Jason, in order to help the Argonauts on their quest.

Come, be ready to perform for me the task I will tell thee of, and I will give thee Zeus' all-beauteous plaything—the one which his dear nurse Adrasteira made for him, while he still lived a child, with childish ways, in the Idaean cave—a well-rounded ball; no better toy will thou get from the hands of Hephaestus. All of gold are its zones, and round each double seams run in a circle; but the stitches are hidden, and a dark blue spiral overlays them all. But if thou shouldst cast it with thy hands, lo, like a star it sends a flaming track through the sky.

Apollonius Rhodius,
Argonautica, Book III
translated by R. C. Seaton,
New Haven/London 1912.

THE FLAMING TRACK

So I asked him why
he was leaving me, and I
don't remember
what he said. I remember the dog
black as his eyelashes
running against her leash, I
remember an amaryllis on its green stalk
red sail of a flower ship, billowing out past its winter deck;
I remember white sheets tacked over
unfurnished apartment windows and the lights
that unfurled on the snow.
I remember footprints,
all the footprints I've left behind me
since then. And the dirty snow
tracked
in on boots
to stain or spot a wooden floor.
And if snow would burn
I would

oh, I surely would,

set those tracks on fire.

SNOW CRASH

I know this title
belongs to somebody else
but my name is
Emerald Ice
and some times
others wear me on their
fingers.

HER GREAT ANGER

The Mailbag Cafe

Dear Craig,

What mutual angers men and women must feel for each other. I began with my anger directed at my mother, thinking that she had driven my father away when he left us for the sea and the life on board ship with other sailors. This was followed by an anger at men, not leaving me for other women, but for men. I never could quite figure out if I felt insulted or simply cheated. From movies and books, I expected women to steal men away from me. But for men to do this also; it seemed like a conspiracy! And of course, all this feeds into my penis envy, my feeling that men have everything. That they are the ones who get to choose. They choose the woman

or other man they will love, while if women do this, they are derided for being aggressive, unattractive, not feminine, not seductive or
sexy.

And men can also choose to be alone. They just seem more Romantic, more alluring, stronger and of course more unobtainably desirable when they stay alone. Other men admire them; women chase them. But when women are alone, they seem pitiful, rejected, old maids, unacceptable in some way. Even their good qualities are overlooked because they are condemned with a spinster-ish, wall flower, weak image. Finally, my father retired from the Navy and divorced my spinster-ish mother and did marry another woman. So, there's my anger at them both, the men and women who stole my father away, or who stole my Jason(s) away from me.

Last comes the anger at the Jasons themselves, those betrayers as I saw them, who left me; but this is hard come by anger, for how can we hate the person we want, so much, to love us? Perhaps as this anger is so hard won, it is more smoldering, more long lasting? My angers about being rejected don't quit or diminish, even though I have been quite happily married to a very loving and desirable man for almost twenty years. I still feel cheated, tricked, deprived by the many Jasons in my life, and I am very angry that this is the ways things are. I still feel great anger towards the men whom I loved who betrayed me in one way or another, even though I have passed far beyond any actual emotional involvement with the men themselves.

The memory of rejection seems indestructible. I have tried to understand this, in the context of my quite successful and happy life; my conclusion is that I need this anger, to keep it alive, to remind me of one of the battles I have spent my life fighting. This battle is the desire to transform the myth of Orpheus, the poet, the lover, in Western civilization into a myth for women as well as for men. If Orpheus can go down to Hell to bring back Eurydice, then Diane can go down to bring back The Motorcycle Betrayer or The Bluemoon Cowboy or The Sheriff of Dry Gulch County.

Like Orpheus, Diane won't be able to bring her lover back. In her case, it's because he's rejected her and won't return. But she, like Orpheus, will become a poet lamenting her loss, and in her case, along with the lament, is another song, one revealing her anger, Her Great Anger, against this death, this loss.

I suppose you already know all of this, but I need to keep re-explaining to myself why the anger is so deep and, most of all, why it cannot go away.

I remain yr Lady of The Flaming Track,

Diane

THE ORIENT EXPRESS

Riding the train to Paris
with a man who was only looking at other men,
stiff table cloth in the dining car
like a groom's shirt, starched
to hold him up—
        Gare du Nord,
        New Year's Eve
Somewhere
there are oysters being shucked with a tool
like your mouth
when you looked at me,
strong and disdainful,
now I know, because
I was a woman. How could
you have married me?
What did you want?
Was Medea this blind when she helped Jason? But
        Jason
wanted something
of her,
the secret of the Golden Fleece. What did you
want from me?

I had nothing but a ragged bag of poems
and the plain face of a woman
who often talked to the moon. If I lived in a world

where I always left
my shoes at the door,
where my chamber was sacred,
would you have known you shouldn't enter?
What rule am I missing? What purpose, what goal
could you
have had?

Like Medea, I escaped in my chariot drawn by dragons,
but not knowing why I the sorceress could not make
you love me, is only an acknowledgment of failure.
What troubles me more,
what does not leave me
even with the peace of old age
is that question
I cannot answer, for it has nothing to do
with magic or enchantment.

Why did you come to me?
What did you want? Why
when you knew I was a woman?
Why, when you knew it was not a woman's face
you daily
wanted to behold?

SHARPE'S MOUTH

thinking about Richard Sharpe, the soldier
played by Sean Bean in the British mini-
series based on novels by Bernard Cornwell
about the Napoleonic wars.

Lovers notice mouths,
like little loaves of bread
they'd like to gobble up.

But that can't
be all of it; the mouth can't really
be more than an entry.

The scars cut on his back from the flogging,
one on his face from the sword,
the pale skin, compacting
a soldier's march through mountains as arid
as old hay—
those images could tell a better story.
But my grey eyes
are on his slicing mouth.

He has to swallow
insults, his mouth twists around
country bread speech, but I see
the man who rejected me insulting him

and being sneered at
with that great tight mouth,
like barbed wire
or simple baling wire holding rounds
of alfalfa. I see the man who hurt me being
cinched up, sliced, crumbled by a
smile rotated taut with pliers-like eyes.
He, the man with that mouth, he'd hold me safe
away from scorn,
with his fence wire grin.

That mouth
doesn't know me, but it honors me
with every twist,
every rifle's sharp crack,
perfectly sighted at even a time-faded,
disappearing target.

THE ASIAN GAY DISCO IN LA

He sits there with his pad of paper
writing in the arc of candlelight supplied by his friends.
    They
revere his priestly activities, though are happier themselves
dancing or flirting or cruising. Occasionally
they borrow a piece of paper—love notes?—
or just sit there, next to him, in safety.

He must look a little like a white American Buddha
with his face oval as a football
and his large plump shoulders breathing softly
over his child-like hands. Will he throw them a
pass, they wonder, or simply smile
lotus-like, engrossed in his handwriting
that to me has always looked a bit like Chinese?

He invites me to come and
tells me I would find it visually exciting,
but I don't think, not being gay, that I really want to go
        there
to look at exotic creatures as if I might be at a zoo.
I am not sure why I feel this way, since I am, above all
        things,
a voyeur and have spent my life looking at everything
as if I were at a zoo or museum or watching a movie.

Perhaps I refrain from accepting his invitation
because I know he wants me
to accept this world as his new family. And for once,
he wouldn't honor
my own scorn of family the way I was allowed to
scorn his blood sister, the con
artist, or satirize his too-pretty mother, make fun
of his engineer dad's
obsession with manliness. What if I found these men I
watched
absurd, ridiculous, pathetic, or dishonest
as I usually find all families?
If I laughed at the failings of
this group of people, or sneered at them,
then I would be considered a bigot,
a bad friend, politically incorrect.

Why does he think a woman
whose husband left her for the gay life
of other men and died of AIDS would want to
watch?

Who is this Zen quarterback? What is his anger
against women
that he wants to share with me
the memory of betrayals and rejections?
Is this a Buddha lesson he doesn't think I've already
learned?

LAGUNA BEACH, RICH MAN'S TOWN

A wave of feeling, déjà vu,
as I drive through the canyon
filled with cypress and fog,
from the highway
to sailor-town San Diego, and see
a few dingy old houses
belonging to the people who lived here
without wealth
from the beginning.

                    Down
to the Pacific.
                    It shines
whatever time of day. This town has always made me
feel
it held secrets; from my childhood
when we came to see wealth we would never have.
And the crafts we called "Art." Now,
of course, it is peopled with ghosts,
all the beautiful homosexual men
who called like sirens
to the man who should never have married me. Michael
        who is only a
square on the AIDS quilt,
still dreaming of the rich and beautiful men

who played Frisbee on the beach.
So removed from that tribe of salt-gathering Indians
the town was named for.

MORNING SHADE

ribbons of tuberose begonias,
especially the yellow,
tear this picture in half. But her
white dress which hangs in the otherwise empty
closet is just flashing lights,
the boat empty and drifting; did someone have an
accident? Oh, John, you fooled me
all those years with your title, I imagined
white shorts, a net, someone furious that he had lost
instead it was The French Revolution, instead
it was her husband baking
scones, instead it was a man who divorced his wife
while eating mango soup, instead it was
crawling in the caves looking for buffaloes,
or homesteading in Alaska without a butter knife.

When Judith comes, she might
bring chanterelles, but this morning I would rather
just sit there, drink my Assam tea. Persephone
doesn't live here any more. She's
in a better neighborhood.

USING ORDINARY WAVES

Using ordinary waves in unusual ways is the secret of quantum theory.

All waves, no matter how exotic, are built on a common plan and take their orders from the same rulebook. Although physicists connect quantum waves with facts in an innovative way, the quantum waves themselves follow the same old-fashioned rules as waves in your bathtub.

Nick Herbert,
Quantum Reality:
Beyond the New Physics

RED BANDANNA

for bad students everywhere

I too like to wear them,
but to me they mean white trousers
after a salty day at the beach, or a busy one on the boat,
yanking bowlines and plying halyards,
while to you, it seems, they wave like a flag on your head,
impetuous, obnoxious, aggressive—
you're the bull wearing your own red flag.

And who knows what has enraged you,
not the color surely, for it's where
your eyes can't see it.
              I see
you come in the door wearing it
and sigh to myself, knowing there will be more snorting
and stomping and unlike Hemingway I couldn't
care less about the running of the bulls,
don't see you as a challenge
but as a mistake,
a middle class man overwhelmed
by this tough Marlboro world you have been
washed with
through TV, and maybe even you think you recognize in
    me

the tough Western sheriff,
maybe you think
you want to shoot it out,
you quick
and me dead.

I don't know
how we could be friends, though you wave that red flag at
        me
as if perhaps you think I'm another bull, or a cow puncher
        who'd ride you;
or perhaps it's just a desperate sign of truce
in your war with a world too big for you right now,
too hostile, too impersonal, too uninterested in you?
I guess I feel something, though not much.

In my cowgirl days, I tried to rescue Sheriff Day
from fascination with guns
and men, and in my tight Western jeans, I married a man
who followed sailors home at night. My ex-husband is a red
        square on the
Aids Quilt,
and Sheriff Day has disappeared into some bullring of his
        own
while I seem now only to be charging at red flags
of artistic and academic deceit.
Still, I am the sailor's daughter, born in the Old West, a girl
        who dreamed of
riding silver-bridled horses and being at the yacht club with
        the rich.
I try to stand or sit, tall and firm in my white jeans
and not to let young bullfighters like you
bother me very much. I like to think I have come through,
survived a world of false seductions.

I too, as I say, like to wear red bandannas, but to me
they are like wearing the sunshine
on my head
or around my neck, and I
didn't think anyone could look at me
with my red bandanna smile,
wide as the Rio Grande River on my face,
which despite the season is as white as a sailor's summer
        uniform,
and not smile back. But you didn't, and I don't know why I
        am surprised.
If I can change,
why can't the world? In the past I would have tried to
win you over, seduce you into poetry or truth. But today,
        you've left me
not smiling, and even less interested than I was before I met
        you
        in bull fights,
                in blood sport,
less willing to smile at you or
        at any young matador or new sailor with my
                once seductive, though never dishonest,
                red-bandanna smile.

CLOVE SHOES

His mouth, with the fragrance of
cinnamon and cloves, never
interested me.

The snow paws of the Blue Spruce
click clack over winter's silvered
linoleum floor,
and I wonder if rose
petals or spiced wine could warm us, that is
if everything were red or gold?

This moon torched
with grainy fire, this sun
leaking oil-prismed
chanterelles, the mushroom
film of a January day, oyster sleek,
no impediment for a snowboarder.

I ask you to
take off your very red hat,
but you unbuckle your belt instead
with its big shield of steel;
no your mouth
never interested me,
never; it was your feet,
like the pads of a leopard, snow
leopard, not that mouth

filled with carnivore teeth
that mouth as bloody
as the moon's dry ice,
hissing and splashing in this glacial
kettle of mulled wine.

DESERT EYES

Far away in the west, the sun was sailing beneath the dark earth, beyond the furthest hills of the Aethiopians; and Night was laying the yoke upon her steeds; and the heroes were preparing their beds by the hawsers. But Jason, as soon as the stars of Helice, the bright-gleaming bear, had set, and the air had all grown still under heaven, went to a desert spot, like some stealthy thief, with all that was needful; for beforehand in the daytime had he taken thought for everything; and Argus came bringing an ewe and milk from the flock; and them he took from the ship. But when the hero saw a place which was far away from the tread of men, in a clear meadow beneath the open sky, there first of all he bathed his tender body reverently in the sacred river; and round him he placed a dark robe, which Hypsiple of Lemnos had given him aforetime, a memorial of many a loving embrace.

Apollonius Rhodius,
Argonautica, translated
by R. C. Seaton,
New Haven/London 1912.

(Jason prepares a sacrifice for the gods before his battle with King Aeetes' bulls and dragon-teeth army)

Though I often go to the desert,
I have only once slept on the ground
with stones encircling our group as if to show
we were married to this spot. I
thought I would look at the Big Dipper,
scooping up the Milky Way, and at Orion the Hunter, his
    red-eyed
starry hilt staring longingly at me from the sky. Dressed in a
    magenta silk
down sleeping bag, all white inside, I watched instead
the way others, couples, bedded down
close to each other and called with friendly
solicitude over to me, the novice camper, "Are you all right
for the night, Diane?"
Whispered assent.
The others had human lovers, but I had the whole desert
    landscape to
embrace:
        the Joshua Trees,
        the yucca flowers,
        the banked all-night fire,
        which one my shy bridegroom?
How to see all this
when I woke up at dawn,
someone already making coffee
and not wish I were
a man?
In my education, men
are always alone,
and they like it. I knew that each husband
or boyfriend, spooned up against a smoky woman
in sleeping bags zipped together,
had looked over at me,
not with desire for my body,

but with longing,
for my single state. Longing. That he could lie alone,
with only the Joshua Tree, the Yucca bell flowers,
the glowing fire pit, and Orion overhead
to keep him safe for his manly life.

HE SAYS

A young man tells me that the
word "Slacker" was coined by his generation
to indicate an opposition to Reaganism as,
for instance, displayed in the neat-suited work-
ethicked
young Republicans who were ambitious for
law and order and monetary success above all
other values
And,
he says
it probably isn't "cool" to use
the word "Slacker" any more. I hear him
bowing to
coolness, I hear him
playing guitar
in the red rock desert
and cherishing his
anger when he cannot bear
even the thought
of shedding blood.
"Face it,"
I tell him,
"human is anger, and also
living beyond anger."

But anger is

blood. It is red with knowing you must
do something to stop or reduce
a sacrilege.
Is he telling me
"Slacker's" an un-cool word
because he himself no longer can identify himself
that way?

He loves his job in a forest service wilderness.
He is angry at men who kill animals, but that anger
is boiling, not cool.
His anger doesn't make
him an animal, doesn't make
him a warrior, it
makes him slack, and hot. Un-cool though it may be, it
doesn't lead him to action.
And I worry when he tells me a word isn't cool any more,
        though I am grateful
        that he is trying to rescue my hot,
        un-slack
        go-getter generation,
        trying to rescue un-cool me.
I wonder if he isn't giving up
the one characteristic his "Slackers" had in common
with my go-getters of civilization:
            the ability to sense irony?
Yes,
    I think,
        ironically,
            he bows to coolness;
                while coolly, I always
                    bow
                    to irony.

LISTENING TO D. H. LAWRENCE'S PANSIES

wanting their eyes, their
broken bones to look at me and draw me
away from surfaces,

wanting their cat's paw petals
to touch my face
like the curl of an eyelash

wanting to go into the woods of Vermont
and cut down a tree,
tell it to try to get up again

wanting to drive up to the artist's studio in the Adirondacks
and throw paint onto a canvas that would reveal
the whole milky way,
as in "the night has a thousand eyes"

wanting to have ridden on a wooden horse to
the home of George Washington
and seen the buttermilk,
the sheets on Martha's bed

and to have waited for a man with big hands
to carry me away wrapped in the American flag,
even before I finished writing a letter
to the ophthalmologist
who prescribed lenses made of pansy faces

wondering what it would be like
to live in a Museum
to cook for Tom Cruise
or to skate on the rings of Saturn

wanting, wanting, wanting
to run through a field of poppies
so white so opaque so bathed in fog
they could replace the ocean

beating death in a
red hood on the Atlantic shore.

SKETCHING ROSES

How many petals
do you draw
before you start skimming
the page with your black ink,
a blackbird flying
away on
Sunday morning?

QUANTUM REALITY #3

QUANTUM REALITY #3 (REALITY IS AN UNDIVIDED WHOLENESS)

The basis for this claim of undivided wholeness is rooted in a curious feature of quantum theory called "phase entanglement." All previously mentioned puzzles of quantum theory concerned the process in which a *single quon* acquires its attributes. The concept of "phase entanglement" arises when we consider how *two or more interacting quons* acquire their attributes.

Whenever two quons meet, so do their representative proxy waves. Their time together is represented by a merging of proxy wave amplitudes, but the phases of the two quons do not come apart. Instead these phases become entangled in such a way that interference effects at quon A depend instantaneously on the disposition of quon B.

Nick Herbert,
*Quantum Reality:
Beyond the New Physics*

WHITE AS SUNDAY SCHOOL SOCKS

And when they are furled like umbrellas,
though white as Sunday socks,
and when they are not on the desert but growing out of a
        pot
placed near my front door, before they have turned
into the huge trumpeting blossoms
I call Moonflowers,
and when their fragrance
is unreleased during the hot summer days, but instead
steals out on to the steps at twilight,
as if they are giant moths who fly away from light
rather than towards it,
                when their aroma is large but delicate
                        like that of a woman whose only perfume is
                                the soap she bathes with, when the scent
expands out to the driveway, and into the air
around the car, as the evening progresses
to darkness, then I am reminded that
each summer
some white flower
comes to dominate
my life. Last year the gardenia
that wouldn't stop flowering,
another summer the begonias, always
so unexpected, like
mushrooms.

It's always been ruby, emerald, sapphire, the colors
that have
drawn me, perhaps
because I myself was
so pale. And diamonds never
my stone, the bridal life never
mine. But summers I wear white like an
engagement ring, it seems. White
flowers, showing me possible destinations,
places
I never before thought
I could go,
inhabit my summers,
like stars that have landed
briefly, on my front yard,
or in the back,
stars, white as my
little girl
Sunday School socks.

ROSES AND SHAME

You never think about the fact that if you sit up
tall enough, you might see
forsythia. This is on a day
when the sky might be blue in the West
but threatening thunder overhead. I never
see pine trees without thinking of
Lake Arrowhead and a cabin where we ate
tongue sandwiches with mayonnaise
and how beauty was all
outside of the car.

There was also the California desert,
looking purple in the distance,
the dusty sage on the edge of the highway
and a knowledge that Palm Springs
was white with movie stars. Who had
ever seen forsythia then?

Who would have known what lilacs were
even if, in the dooryard,
they might have been said
to bloom? It was roses
and bougainvillea, calla lilies, lantana,
camellias with their heavy bruised faces as they aged,
and my shame,
oh ugly little girl without a daddy,

with an old mother,
without Shirley Temple curls,
who wet the bed.

Not a little Rose, just a
little girl, how common, how silly,
how lucky you were to have
the real people
in books
and not to have
to live like *The Purple Rose of Cairo*,
reeling without common flowers, such as
the golden poppies blundering all over the brown hills
of Southern California.

PANSIES

Didn't have any
this year.
No thoughts either;
that's why I am feeling
so calm.

WAITING FOR THE MORNING GLORIES

Each year,
no matter what seeds, out of
the gold foil packets like expensive gifts
from Parks, or the plain
brown wrappers of Burpees,
or the butcher paper white of Vermont Bean & Seed,
or even
the magazine cover packets from Meijer's Thrifty Acres,
the trumpet flowers,
blue as lapis,
are scarcer and scarcer. The packets
I might plant
for one or two days of a dozen flowers.

This year,
in one spot I planted three times before I even
got
one crop, religiously soaking the rat-turd hard seeds
overnight. And finally,
some vines came along
but so did autumn, and I thought of the frauds of
my life; the gardener, the good cook, the bird watcher, the
daughter.

Everyone says that if you plant zucchini
you will wind up with enough squash to write a

cookbook, but
each year
we're lucky if we have seven or eight,
total,
before the squash worms decimate the plants,
and you all know
that only sparrows come to our feeder,
I married a man who,
at the time,
preferred Campbell's pork & beans to a cassoulet.
And in the garden my childhood memory of morning glories
as weeds
seems also to have its contradictions.

You see why I'm writing this.
Because last week,
all of a sudden,
almost October, the glories started
to bloom. Old vines,
and new ones, some on the trellises, some hovering
at the base of the chimney,
and some scattered among bending, broken sunflower
stalks. Blue
as the Pacific Ocean I long for, here in the midwest,
blue as those "heaps of beads poured into my breast
and clacking together in my elbows," blue as
Monday, and blue as
roses are not supposed to be. They shone
through the rain, they glowed in the
fog of the mornings, and they've transformed
the silky grey mourning trousers of this fall
so far with a feeling that maybe I haven't
understood, yet,
this common flower. And more

a promise that the end
of a season
may surprise you
with its beauty. Something final
besides just death?

YELLOW TULIPS & THE QUESTION OF BEAUTY

Did she ever get
her hands dirty? Well, probably, yes. That
surely isn't the issue; it's whether or not
she ever had to look in the mirror
and recognize an awkward face, dumpy features,
unshapely arms? And then, why
wouldn't she still want the same things,
everyone wants,
beautiful or ugly?

It all comes down to
equality.
And maybe no one ever steadies
the balance for long. I want
her to lose something
for her beautiful face, whereas
she simply wants to beat me because
she's better, or is it
more beautiful? She wants it all
and will get it.

Two cardinals, a blue jay,
some purple finches
and a lot of nondescript sparrows.

After all, which birds do you
prefer
to come to your feeder?
And why do the neighbors' tulips always look so
much better than
ours?

MORNING GLORIES

Every year
the trumpet blows louder.

MEDEA,
THE ARGONAUT ROSE

But soon he appeared to her longing eyes, striding along loftily, like Sirius coming from ocean, which rises fair and clear to see, but brings unspeakable mischief in flocks; thus did Aeson's son [Jason] come to her, fair to see, but the sight of him brought love-sick care. Her heart fell from out of her bosom, and a dark mist came over her eyes, and a hot blush covered her cheeks. And she had no strength to lift her knees backwards or forwards, but her feet beneath were rooted to the ground; and meantime all her hand-maidens had drawn aside. So they two stood face to face without a word, without a sound, like oaks, or lofty pines, which stand quietly side by side on the mountains when the wind is still; then again when stirred by the breath of the wind, they murmur

ceaselessly; so they two were destined to tell out their
tale stirred by the breath of Love.

Apollonius Rhodius,
Argonautica, Book III,
translated by R. C. Seaton,
New Haven/London 1912.

HER FRUSTRATION

She's sending a message she can't utter. This man
wants to whisk her up with his magnetic hands
like the points of discarded nails she says her lover picked up
at a partially built house they were
exploring. And she would like that too,
to be gathered into his enfolding hands,
for she keeps talking about walls and wanting to be
contained, to be held. "Structure," she calls it,
but it's because she's afraid to say
"why don't you hold me
the way the man I live with
never holds me, even though he holds nails
in his hand?"

And this man to whom she cannot utter these words
himself is afraid to say anything except, "yes those points,
I'd like to hold those nails which you call 'points'
in my hand, scoop them up and think about
taking them home, building
something interesting
with them."
But

I am the only one who knows the point
of what either one of you
is saying.
You live in the same house, and pretend

to love other people, but I hear you,
I hear you, and think
"what can I offer?"
knowing that long ago
I exchanged direct utterance
for speaking to someone other than
the one I loved. My life now
has a subtext that surprises even me!
And I too would love
to gather up a handful of nails
some time, and see who would look at me and say,
"I want to hold them in my
hands."

I am quite sure there would be no one,
not even my husband,
yet I cannot bear to think this. Instead, I think of
what my answer would be:
"though I could not give anyone a whole
handful
of nails, I could offer one."
When I passed over
one of those nails, it would change into
a ring, not one of the rings of Saturn, but a ring
like a sign of majesty.
Something more than friendship,
—what she who is frustrated wants to offer both men—
though, of course,
as she knows,

these points, the nail, this ring,
even if contained,
can never easily be
defined.

138

Dear Jonathan,

As you know, I continue to look for reasons why aging itself offers interesting additions to one's life. Am always hard-pressed to find them; however, one aspect of my life that has changed as I've aged is that I become more interested in other people's lives, and in some cases more interested in their lives than my own. As a long-time poet narcissist, this surprises me.

I also continue to try to find reasons why my life in academia can be considered an artistic plus, when it is so obvious that contemporary academia is just another business, and business (far more than the military) has always been the enemy to my generation of intellectuals and artists. But what I find is not only that I love the act of analyzing poetry and presenting contemporary poetry in the context of myth and history, but also that I love the dramas that occur in my classroom and office, often between students with me as the only observer. Voyeur, in some cases, as I feel that I am observing things they think they are hiding.

This sequence of poems, starting with "Her Frustration," along with a number of other poems in recent years was generated by watching what I thought of as a subtext to a poetry tutorial I was offering. Of course, these hidden dramas interest me because I myself feel so mesmerized still by my failures in male-female discourse, in winning over my own romantic objects, and of course, like Medea, in making the men I desired during my own youth love me as much as I wanted or desired them.

One of the features of aging is that you lose your sexuality—that is, in the eyes of others. This is a punishment for many of us—especially women, as we need to be seen sexually, to be desired by men. The other side of the coin, though, is that when one loses the ability to inspire desire in others, he/she becomes safe. Thus people can tell us stories without fear that we ourselves any longer desire to be part of the story. And if you are as good a secret-keeper as I am, you hear many stories, though often in disguised forms. For, aren't we all secret-keepers? Don't we all leave something untold?

I remain yr Lady of Secret East Lansing Light,

DW

p.s. a contemporary fashion that has totally eluded me is why anyone would want to paint her fingernails blue! I can somewhat respond to black or brown lipstick and nail polish, but blue? Blue somehow emphasizes how ugly most nails are. Or maybe blue is truly the color of death, for me, not black or white or red, any of which often symbolize it.

DW

BLUE NAILS

Hands as little as the leaves of the sapling Honey Locust
    Tree,
and he looks at them as if he knows how
they would feel, landing kitten-like on his shoulders.
With her small fingernails painted light blue
and looking pagan to me,
as if she worshipped Oak Trees
and spoke only superstitions,
she reaches out to offer me a piece of paper
and the little blue nails
are like bits of broken eggshell,
tumbled among the departing leaves.
He has given her
everything he can, even spreading his arms out
wide, imitating crucifixion,
and she imagines that he's a scarecrow
standing there with her in a roadside park,
next to a local cornfield,
where they've stopped the car to smoke
and talk. Her little blue nails
must not look like anything the movies ever
offered as seductive, and her smoking hands not like
those of a Patricia Neal in *The Fountainhead*, but like
a kindergartner's hands, decorated with the glitter of broken
    robin's egg
shells. Yet those are the nailed hands

he'd like to hold in his own hands,
gather to him,
build something with them.
But right now, there he is, yes
he's the one, nailed
to the cross of her pagan nature, wispy, dancing
over the marsh in a blue flame, he transfixed,
nailed there in love with her little
blue nails, Her hands,
she says, belong to another
man.

Of course, I find that
very hard to believe. Why, if that other love weren't dead,
would she
paint her fingernails
blue? Broken eggshell
blue?

CRUCIFIED

And now that words have passed the point where they could
ever have become song, now that words have become
so physical, so pointed,
like nails, and they've both
filled their hands with the big tenpenny
kind, they have to stop
talking to each other,
at least in this room, at least
with me licking my whiskers
like a big green cat. He's already offered
himself to her, though his words are building
quite another kind of structure,
not a house,
but perhaps a temple
to loneliness;
and she still doesn't know what to do
with more than one lover;
She's not prepared to believe
this man with calluses on his palms from rowing
is a good replacement for her perfect man,
the one who doesn't really love her very much,
the one who dances in a room
ignoring her while she paints her fingernails blue
and thinks of vampires. And she is much better
at saying "no" than anything
else.

There is no reason
to think of sacrifice or the passion of Christ
in this story, but nevertheless
there was a carpenter originally, one
with a handful of nails, and
a woman who thought longingly
of what they might build together. But she
is afraid now to be in the same room
with the builder, and her
mirrorman doesn't even know or care
about Stevens' topaz rabbit or emerald cat,
the green and walking night that
ended for both of them,
though he doesn't know it yet,
without song.

The unusual demands Bell's theorem makes on reality give us our clearest picture to date of the irreducible strangeness of the quantum world.... Bell's theorem reads: The quantum facts plus a bit of arithmetic require that reality be non-local. In a local reality, influences cannot travel faster than light. Bell's theorem says that in any reality of this sort, information does not get around fast enough to explain the quantum facts: reality must be non-local.

Nick Herbert,
Quantum Reality:
Beyond the New Physics

BEING A MILLIONAIRE

She looks like
Grace Kelly, plays
volleyball
with a silver brace on her knee,
tells me they're called "don johns,"
and I start thinking about the possible prisons
of language. Her grandfather founded
a steel company, she's the chrome-edged
sister to her traffic-ticketed brother.
I tell her that she trusts metal too much,
that even money
backed by silver or gold
is theoretical because it doesn't have
intrinsic value. Gold and silver are valuable because
they are scarce. "We do not save or spend money because it
        is beautiful,
do we?" I ask.
"This book," I say
"contains something that you want for
itself." As she does,
as I hope I do.
But her young sapphire eyes are older than my steely ones,
with the many injuries of her athletic life and reflect
her brother's accusations against her father
that he gives her everything, his delinquent son
nothing. Interesting that she has

the money, but her brother wants it; she has
the body timed to athletic speed and precision yet she
also sees something beyond
that perfection. Who ever thought
such a princess would show up at this Land Grant
institution? Her brother driving the sports car recklessly
around the curves, skidding past the rails,
and I watching the movie
that might be made in Monte Carlo,
(*Bonjour, Tristesse*)
of her life?

THE OARSMAN

And their arms shone in the sun like flame as the ship sped
on; and ever their wake gleamed white far behind, like a path
seen over a green plain.

> Apollonius Rhodius,
> *Argonautica, Book I,*
> translated by R. C. Seaton,
> New Haven/London 1912.

He is on the school crew team
though in winter they have only indoor, non-marine
        training,
lifting weights or rowing dry machines.
And though he's blond and slim, with a heft of shoulder,
he doesn't look as I
would expect an oarsman to look, that is
I can't imagine him seating himself down on the Argos,
each bench there holding two rowers,
all men descended from Gods, or at least mortal rulers,
all would-be heroes,
chiefs and
the sons of chiefs.
His sandpapery skin; his used-looking longish hair; his fearful
lack of poise, as if he's always embarrassed by his lack

of class—he's one who makes me want to look
to see
if this might transform some time
into beauty. I think: no.
Though I am often wrong about such things.

He certainly isn't like Jason, their leader,
whom the Greek poet thus described,
"And as Apollo goes forth from some fragrant shrine ... in
        such beauty moved Jason
                through the throng of people."
In fact, all the Argonauts are constantly compared to
stars, or other shining things.
It is of course Apollo
who is Jason's god.
But I can't imagine this young midwestern man
actually in
their company,
though perhaps he thinks of himself
like that sometimes. Perhaps
when he is rowing, as the Argonauts rowed, his arms
        seem
to him
like flames?

I only see him hiding
in the back of a room, nestling as close as he can
to a sweet little Athena,
with a close helmet of dark hair
guarding her against his need. Her mind in fact,
only focused on another curly head,
forbidden, not like flame
but a night cloaked kiss, almost un-given,
also a story with islands and women left behind, also a story
        of betrayal,

149

her married Jewish lover who will not leave his wife for
her. As I say, this rower does not think of himself usually
in a golden company of heroes. He is awkward and he
has no sense of why women
might cherish him. He's not in the helm
nor sitting on the divine board laid into the Argos from a
      Dodonian oak,
the seat where Herakles and Hylas are at the center of men
      who do not care for women
and guide the quest.

I don't know
the rower's story, only that he told us
of a sensuous encounter with a woman
in an aquarium store,
about how fearful he was that he could not be perceived as
      a lover;
but I wondered at the time
if in fact he didn't love a mermaid,
not a woman, or if he himself
doubted that he could be a manly lover?
I find myself impressed now, that he cannot see himself as
      Jason,

for I cannot look at men without wondering if they are
      able to
love without betrayal.

I see him foundering
at the back of the room, as if he's in the key seat for guiding
      a boat,
and the girl who might be his goddess
only looked to for comfort, not romance.
She, for her other longings, not seeing him either

even though his rowing arms might be on fire.
In fact, no one perceiving him
as Jason—his being an oarsman
the only connection to that betraying hero—and

isn't that
just as well?

HER CURLY LOCKS AND
THE STRAIGHT-HAIRED ROWER

She jumps for a volley ball shot
and tendrils of her curly pancake-brown hair
steam out and then settle around her ears.
He's not watching,
the rower, training in another gym,
with a syrup of sinewy muscles embracing
his shoulders.
Instead it's her boyfriend, with the straight
shoulder-length hair that streams out
like a wake behind his head,
straight hair that puffs and furls like a sail, whereas her curly
hair would turn into frizzled bacon, if she ran a dry brush
        through it
before breakfast.

In fact, she only loves
men with straight hair, and has
a predilection for big shoulders,
and that description fits both men. But she
doesn't really care about any of that more than
poetry. In fact, she wishes one of them
would write love poems to her
rather than dry rowing in the exercise machine,
standing in the shower with her
after they've both sweated through men's and women's

volley ball games. She's been thinking of Samson,
while I've been looking beyond hair
to the power a lover has.

After making love with her long-haired
boyfriend, she doesn't know if
breakfast is a meal for lovers or betrayers. She
doesn't know
how to put love and sex, straight and curly hair,
or her mother's meals and pages of poetry
together, until I say "Have you ever heard
of courtly love?" Well, she has,
but never thought that it might be
related to a man who
rows and writes poems about
other women, the man she wishes were
watching her after the pancake, syrup and bacon breakfast,
or when she's jumping for the net,
or how
imagination
might be better than a cup of coffee
in the morning, or might
even turn any game into a volley
with love.

COSTA RICAN COFFEE

I scissor open the brown and white pack
and instantly the smell of morning
fills this kitchen. The steaming water drips through
the maker like a lover moving next
to your sleeping body in the night and putting an
arm around your torso so that you feel as if
your body is as beautiful as the Venus de Milo. How lucky
you are in this loveless world
to have a cup of coffee to start the day,
its brown tongue presses against your lips
until you feel their redness.
You aren't in a movie, you aren't
rich or happy, you aren't
even doing something meaningful with your life. It's just
a new day and you remember that
the arms which held you
during the night
have been missing for centuries.
You know
nothingness:
smell and taste its
topaz mouth.

AND HERE
THEY FOUND CIRCE

And here they found Circe bathing her head in the salt sea-spray, for sorely had she been scared by the visions of the night. With blood her chambers and all the walls of her palace seemed to be running, and flame was devouring all the magic herbs with which she used to bewitch strangers whoever came; and she herself with murderous blood quenched the flowing flame, drawing it up in her hands; and she ceased from deadly fear. Wherefore when morning came she rose, and with sea-spray was bathing her hair and her garments.

Apollonius Rhodius,
Argonautica, Book IV,
translated by R. C. Seaton,
New Haven/London 1912.

WET SUIT

for the Silver Surfer

He sleeps on black sheets
and rises at dawn. Black-suited
he sculpts his way into the surf, his board no
wider than he is, two narrow
shadows that stand up
to the curl;
one woman walking on
the beach sees them
with the eye
of a blackbird.

THE EMERALD SKIN

The color of an orange has absolutely no correlation with the maturity of the flesh and juice inside. An orange can be sweet and ripe as it will ever be and still glisten like an emerald in the tree. Cold—coolness, rather—is what makes an orange orange. In some parts of the world, the weather never gets cold enough to change the color; in Thailand, for example, an orange is a green fruit, and traveling Thai often blink with wonder at the sight of oranges with the color of flame.

John McPhee,
Oranges

In the groves
you stole it

In the groves
you lifted an edge
of sparkling orange peel

In the groves
you saw it
until it disappeared.

In the groves
it dazzled you;

then it disappeared.
In the groves
you peeled the green skin
before it vanished.

In the groves
you saw it
turn to orange

In the groves
you ate it
and it vanished

In the groves
gold finches flew out
of the oranges.

Gold and black spiders wove
their webs around
the oranges.

Black and yellow snakes
sipped their juice.

Swallowtail butterflies
visited their blossoms
and black and yellow bees
also tasted oranges.

In the groves
you saw them.
In the groves
you stole them.
In the groves

you watched them disappear.
Invisible,
The King of Spain,
The King of Spain,
first you saw him,
then you disappeared,
The Golden King of Spain,
stepping out of an emerald skin.

HURRICANE INSOMNIA

*a meditation on Richard Wilbur's
"Love Calls Us to the Things of
This World"*

When the night taps on the glass
of my sleep, and in the dark I brush past
down comforters, puffy as birds look when huddled away
from a storm, to see
who's there, I find no one but myself, as tall as
sugar cane, but no wind.
The island of four a.m.
makes me shiver, I put on a heavy
white Irish sweater that I've mended and mended to keep
its comfort whole, and though outside I know that the
sunflowers
are bending almost to the earth with autumn
so that I also need wool socks as soft as gardenias
on my bare feet before I descend
the stairs, it's not the fatigue
of sleep disturbance that I carry with me.
Like the lightning clusters of gypsy peppers
ripening in their late season pots, I feel tight,
ready. I've heard the voice of a fifties poem saying, "Love
calls us to the things of this world" so clearly in my ear
that I could not remain lying there in the inner warmth of
my marriage,
cuddled, cosseted, a peaceful woman

161

of middle age. Instead, sound on the glass,
the swish of linen, my padded body
all combine to say to me, "we're here, we're
here."

I do not listen for Christ
in that voice, or think that I might ever
hear angels. What I hear is the soft turning of pages,
the clink of my cup of steaming green tea
against its huge saucer, the hard edge of my mind
drawing a line that is not
on a washline pulley holding crackling bed
sheets, but instead extends like a phone line into eternity
where sometimes, when we have been quiet enough,
or slept with an empty enough mind,
we can visit. I don't need my pillow, though I always
carry it downstairs when these body storms
awaken me, usually hoping to return
to sleep, trick myself with yellow-shaded mission light.
Tonight, something called me down the stairs
to read that old book on my shelves since college, and think
     that if it
weren't
for the title, the poem would never
have stayed in my mind.

Love always called me
in ways that author could not have understood, which is
     why
his words are even more precious, since they clearly come
from a place even he doesn't know
very well. At times like this I think I understand
what my education has been all about. Not throwing the
     stick

at the venomous
gold snake in Sicily, as Lawrence belatedly did,
not waking to the earthiness of Wilbur's Italy,
nor having been the Eskimo re-birthed inside of Kinnell's
    trophy bearskin,
but like all of them,
knowing that I have been in the presence of something
I could worship, were I the
worshipping kind.

THE BAKER'S WIFE

She is tiny as a butter knife
and as if she were some dainty pastry, she
often wears lace or hugs silver
next to her cheek.
No children, but in the kitchen, a big red and blue Macaw,
a living room full of yellow and blue parakeets
which she claims all talk to her while she reads poetry
and drinks coffee from a doll-sized cup.

If I met her in the library, I'd
never think she were married to a dough
man. And if in fact I saw her husband on the street,
with his torso slim as a French baguette,
and his long-fingered hands which don't seem like paddles
or even hooks, but more like those
of a man on a tropical terrace drinking rum,
I wouldn't guess
that either of them go fishing
in the Rocky Mountains on their vacation,
or that they avidly read a Star Trek
fanzine.

Whether deep reality is truly non-local or not could be settled in an instant by the discovery of a single superluminal signal. If the world is in truth bound together everywhere by faster-than-light connections, can we exploit these links to send superfast messages to our friends? Such an accomplishment would not only directly validate Bell's conclusion, it would initiate a new era for humankind, making us masters of space and time.

Nick Herbert,
Quantum Reality:
Beyond the New Physics

WHERE HAVE I SEEN HER BEFORE?

Her voice is like good custard, *crème brulée* perhaps, and she uses one hand always extended as if she's balancing herself. She holds in her other hand the salamander iron, right out of an old French kitchen that, hot and ready to scald the top of the dessert, Julia brought into TV kitchens. I wanted to mention that this woman is probably not a cook, that she was a child math prodigy, that she has eyes like blue equations.

Yet how do we know what we'll be able to contribute to the world—cooks, mathematicians, breeders of whippets? Chef Child brought so much to American kitchens, but she claims that she'll be remembered for only one thing. She believes her contribution to American cooking is the small blow torch. Because of Julia, along with the mixers and Cuisinarts, we now need a blow torch, to take the place of the old wood-fire-heated salamander, in our inventory of kitchen appliances.

Last Christmas Judith Minty asked for a small chainsaw for Christmas. I confirmed recently that I could not be happy without bread, cheese and wine. The math prodigy asked me, opening wide her scallop eyes and speaking like *crème brulée*, if I could tell her who The King of Spain was. "Yes," I answered, "he comes from fairy tales." But it seemed more important today, somehow, to figure out why I thought I recognized a name like a constellation? When did I ever eat *crème brulée* that was seared the way this woman's voice burned through to my past?

CRAIG'S LASAGNA

Can't stop thinking about
those beautiful noodles
and the emerald green pesto
while others
in LA were roller blading their way
onto the Pasadena freeway.

[CIRCE] LONGED TO HEAR THE VOICE

[Circe] longed to hear the voice of the maiden, her kins-woman, as soon as she saw that she had raised her eyes from the ground. For all those of the race of Helios were plain to discern, since by the far flashing of their eyes they shot in front of them a gleam of gold. So Medea told her all she asked—the daughter of Aestes of the gloomy heart, speaking gently in the Colchian tongue, both of the quest and the journeyings of the heroes, and of their toils in the swift con-tests, and how she had sinned through the counsels of her much-sorrowing sister, and how with the sons of Phrixus she had fled afar from the tyrannous horrors of her father; but she shrank from telling of the murder of Apsyrtus.

Apollonius Rhodius,
Argonautica, Book IV,
translated by R.C. Seaton,
New Haven/London 1912.

NIGHT CITY

The streets are like an old library
with uncluttered tables where I once read
The Secret Garden.
Uncomfortable chairs, stiff as male relatives,
the feeling that the past
is well-built in oak,
though not particularly beautiful.
But who
cares? The words hiss
behind our eyes
like the memory of daytime traffic.
The stoplights work at the same pace and
with the same sequence at night,
while almost no one
but we five walkers
waits for them, crosses, or follows their directions.

We are looking for a bar where we
can order a bottle of wine,
sit and talk, perhaps even about books we
are reading. We don't think much
about the secrets that might
be locked into the
night-empty buildings,
or for that matter
our own secrets.

We are simply a group of friendly acquaintances
in a city where none of us lives.
In a sense, we have all entered through
our closets, or a locked garden gate,
and in fact would feel no connection at all
if we were together in the day light.
It is the nighttime of words that connects us,
as if it leads us to Narnia,
Dr. Doolittle's realm, or the Emerald City.

I like this night city because it seems so much like
the old Carnegie-style library I frequented when I grew up
in Whittier, California. Being an adult doesn't change
        things.
These cotton summer-shirted strangers
can only relate to me through words,
oh yes, words,
so much better, I discovered, than an action or
a touch, or even
love. These street lamps have just turned into
the magnolia tree with incandescent blossoms that shaded
the year-round emerald
entrance to
"Children's Books" at the Whittier Public Library.
I am still the reader wearing my cap of darkness,
never letting go
of the stories while,
all my life I remain invisible, a secret garden of neon,
orange
California poppies,
secretly blooming
outside
everybody's window.

IRISH MOON

not in the bathtub on stork legs,
not in the long fringes of my silk scarf,
not in copper clad teapot of China Black,
not in the mullioned or glazed windows of my house,
nowhere on the shelves of hand made books

you won't find it,
anything like it,
the Maud moon,
the Irish moon, the
dancing bawd of poetry.

We dusted.
It's not there.

OLD EMBROIDERED CHINESE ROBES IN
THE ANN ARBOR MUSEUM

Sometimes I think that museums
are just closets for the rich.
Opening a door
the intimate scent wafts out. Aramis
or Chloe. Imagine
sleeping with the wearers
of these paintings? or watching them dress
in the morning?

Stretched and pinned against the wall, like a fan
and not a garment, is an old
embroidered Chinese robe,
as brilliant as this summer's urn
filled with white and red
impatiens, flowers
waterfalling up and over its edges.

A silk robe.
There's one in my closet of baby
shoes and old fountain pens.
On its back, an
embroidered dragon also coils and froths
to remind me of my summer
excesses and failures
with a man I loved.

Like those other robes stretched against
the museum wall
my own robe, unworn, has become
an artifact
but there are no collectors to examine it,
wonder what life was like
for the wearer. No one to ask,
"how much does it cost
to live
a complete life?"

It is unused beauty.
I have feared wearing it,
not wanted to stain it with water
or carelessly spilled tea.
I ask myself what the difference is
between my closet and these museum walls
and know I will not find an answer

no matter how carefully I spread the tea leaves
stranded at the bottom of my cup.

REMEMBERING THE PACIFIC

I don't remember seeing it at night. It would look like
the groom at a wedding, in his black tuxedo
with only a crest of foaming shirtfront.
Of course when I
lived just a block away from the ocean
in Laguna Beach, or in Solano Beach, California
I must have seen it often
at night. But I have a hard time
pulling the image to my eyes, the way
when someone you love dies,
your husband, your father,
you suddenly realize you can't remember
his face.

It panics you, it frightens you, it
most of all
makes you sad, then angry;
what is the matter with your mind,
your mind that once was like a history book
filled with everything that had ever been recorded?
Night is when you stayed away, if you
were going to
stay away.
Night is when the oranges rolled out the door,
or the spoons rattled in the drawer. Night
is when the cup emptied itself, night is when

books broke their leather bindings, and toothbrushes
disappeared.

At night, the ocean swallowed everything
until the whole world was invisible. At night,
my father betrayed my mother, my husband slept with
        others,
and I could only look at the ocean and be fearful
that nothing in it was an orange, a rose,
a glove, a book, or
anything I could count on to take care
of me. Not even the white crests of groom's-shirt waves, so
        often
imagined in Classical literature as horses. No
white horse, or even a surfer on an old board, coming
out of those waves to carry me
to safety. No I can't
remember what the ocean looked like
at night, though I do think
of the ocean
all the time.

IMAGINING POINT DUME

for the Motorcycle Betrayer

There are so many photographs of that curve of rocky beach
like a scallop shell itself, only reversed,
the green and blue striped ocean like the tray
of this calcified fan, the white coast,
my hand that holds Athena's shield,
this shell without its meat
of pinkish flesh

California motels, pink stucco,
with palm trees and the aura of World War II
populate movies and any flashes I have of my childhood,
but you were not there, you were glowering
at your father on Long Island,
you were wearing leather jackets and smoking cigarettes
and looking out of your hooded Clint Eastwood Hungarian
        eyes,
I only remember the big hand, cupped over a match
lighting your Lucky Strike.

And in those pink-tiled bathrooms constructed
in every housing development house
in the early fifties, we looked in steamy mirrors
that told us we weren't beautiful enough.

The mirror in the living room with pink flamingos painted
        at its
edges, also told us about our inadequacies.
But mirrors were unnecessary
because we had the ocean,
because we walked the dusty roads past the irrigation
        ditches,
filled with imported water,
because we washed our hair in water
filled with the minerals of the desert. Oh, the mirror

only added to the gleam of truth
that water represented in our lives.
Water which I imagine
as the Pacific Ocean
which is of course just
beyond the trees
of my backyard here in Michigan. I have carried it
with me
all my days
that mirror
reflecting the pinkish scallop shells,
            the pink flamingoes,
            the pink stucco
            of my childhood
like a pink Las Vegas dawn,
composed of neon light.

EPILOGUE

MUSTACHES AND BEARDS

for John Landry, a gesture

which aisle was it? near the brooms?
canned vegetables where I was looking for hearts of palm?
or over where the summer barbecue displays were set up?
    just a fat girl, no
a woman in stretch pants and T-shirt, arms like soccer balls,
super market shoes/ my eye
moves up looking for grill brushes and
rushes past her face, grizzled like an old dog, not the
    sharksilk of
summer tanned skin, but on her cheeks, like the pile
on velour sofas, hirsute, like grass on smooth hills,
almost a beard, dark shadow over the mouth. She's used to
turning her face away, or being stared at.
I don't linger on it.

I've seen a young woman turning into a werewolf
right here in Meijer's Thrifty Acres
in mid-Michigan. Nothing on the shelves now
looks good to me. This is where poverty shops,
and I thought we lived in a world where
no one had to have bad teeth any more,
or moles dangling from their noses
or such messed up hormones that they
grew hair in the wrong places before they were twenty. I
    haven't seen

Walt Whitman in this supermarket, just this girl whom
        someone
should take care of, medically,
and it makes my well-fed, overindulged life,
this life of books and poetry, movies and three course meals
        with friends
seem somewhat askew to me. But what could I do
for her werewolf face by giving up any
of those things?
This is what many of us in America in 1996 think about
daily. I don't know if we should, but we could

reduce it
to mustaches and beards.

Printed January 1998 in Santa Barbara
& Ann Arbor for the Black Sparrow Press by
Mackintosh Typography & Edwards Brothers Inc.
Text set in Bembo by Words Worth.
Design by Barbara Martin.
This first edition is published in paper wrappers;
there are 250 hardcover trade copies;
100 hardcover copies have been numbered & signed
by the poet; & 26 lettered copies with an
original holograph poem have been handbound
in boards by Earle Gray & are signed by the poet.

Photo: Robert Turney

DIANE WAKOSKI was born in Whittier, California in 1937 and educated at U.C. Berkeley. She has published twenty full-length collections of poems and many other slim volumes. Her most recent collections from Black Sparrow are *Emerald Ice: Selected Poems 1962–1987* which won the Poetry Society of America's William Carlos Williams Award in 1988, *Medea the Sorceress* (1990), *Jason the Sailor* (1993) and *The Emerald City of Las Vegas* (1995). She is currently Writer in Residence at Michigan State University.